THE
WORLD'S
STUPIDEST
SIGNS

The majority of these signs were spotted by the Publisher. However, we should also like to thank readers of our previously published *Please Take Advantage of the Chambermaid and other Silly Signs*, who sent in their stupid signs to us. We should also like to acknowledge the *New Scientist* magazine's Feedback page, where some of the signs included in this book have appeared. If you have any signs you would like to send to us for a future collection, please e-mail them to **jokes@michaelomarabooks.com**

THE WORLD'S STUPIDEST SIGNS

Michael O'Mara Humour

First published in Great Britain in 2000 by
Michael O'Mara Books Limited
9 Lion Yard
Tremadoc Road
London SW4 7NQ

A CIP catalogue record for this book is available from the
British Library

ISBN 1-84317-170-8

21 23 25 27 29 30 28 26 24 22 20

Edited by Bryony Evens

Designed and typeset by Design 23

www.mombooks.com

Printed and bound in Britain
by Cox and Wyman Ltd, Reading, Berks

WEARING
THIS
GARMENT
DOES NOT
ENABLE
YOU
TO FLY

On a child's Superman costume

ICE
CREAM
TOILETS

On a campsite

WE DO NOT TEAR YOUR CLOTHING WITH MACHINERY. WE DO IT CAREFULLY BY HAND.

In a dry cleaner's

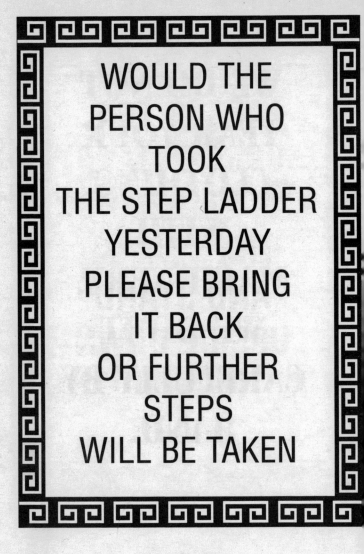

WOULD THE
PERSON WHO
TOOK
THE STEP LADDER
YESTERDAY
PLEASE BRING
IT BACK
OR FURTHER
STEPS
WILL BE TAKEN

In a factory

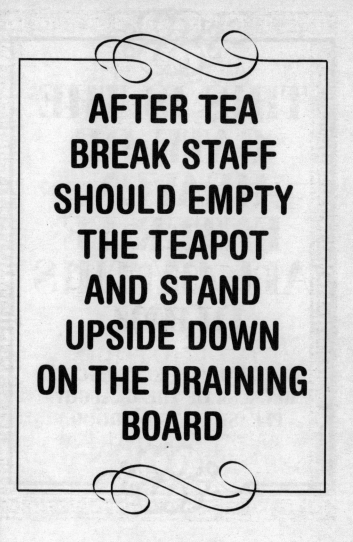

**AFTER TEA
BREAK STAFF
SHOULD EMPTY
THE TEAPOT
AND STAND
UPSIDE DOWN
ON THE DRAINING
BOARD**

In an office

THIS IS THE GATE OF HEAVEN. ENTER YE ALL BY THIS DOOR.

(THIS DOOR IS KEPT LOCKED BECAUSE OF THE DRAUGHT– PLEASE USE SIDE DOOR.)

On a church door

CAUTION:
AUTOMATIC
DOOR
PUSH TO
OPERATE

**On the entrance door
to an office building**

THURSDAY NIGHT POTLUCK SUPPER PRAYERS AND MEDICATION TO FOLLOW

Notice in a parish magazine

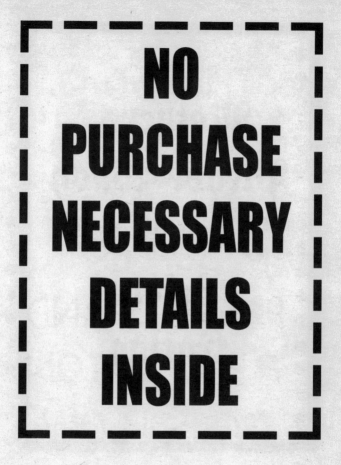

NO PURCHASE NECESSARY

DETAILS INSIDE

On several different snack wrappers

Mothers, Please Wash Your Hans Before Eating

English sign in a German café

THE TOWN HALL IS CLOSED UNTIL OPENING. IT WILL REMAIN CLOSED AFTER BEING OPENED. OPEN TOMORROW

Sign outside a new town hall which was to be opened by the Prince of Wales

SLOW CATTLE CROSSING NO OVERTAKING FOR THE NEXT 100 YRS

Seen at the side of a Sussex road

ONE HOUR PHOTOS READY IN 20 MINUTES

Outside a shop in Brixton, London

WARNING: HIGH IN SODIUM

On a container of salt

SAFETY FIRST PLEASE PUT ON YOUR SEAT BELT PREPARE FOR ACCIDENT

Sign in a Japanese taxi

NOT TO BE REMOVED FROM CREWE STATION

On a luggage trolley at Singapore airport

**SWIMMING POOL
SUGGESTIONS
OPEN 24 HOURS
LIFEGUARD
ON DUTY
8AM TO 8PM
DROWNING
ABSOLUTELY
PROHIBITED**

Sign at a resort in the Philippines

WE CAN REPAIR ANYTHING.

**(PLEASE KNOCK HARD
ON THE DOOR –
THE BELL
DOESN'T WORK)**

Sign on a repair shop door

DO NOT TURN UPSIDE DOWN

Printed on the BOTTOM of a tiramisu dessert box

TOILET OUT OF ORDER PLEASE USE FLOOR BELOW

In a toilet in a London office block

OPEN SEVEN DAYS A WEEK

(EXCEPT MONDAYS)

Sign at a New York restaurant

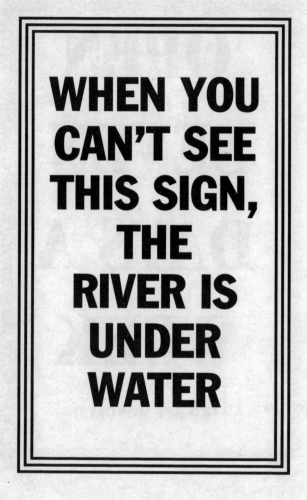

WHEN YOU CAN'T SEE THIS SIGN, THE RIVER IS UNDER WATER

Sign in a country lane

WANTED: EJECTION SEAT TESTER INVOLVES A SMALL AMOUNT OF TRAVELLING

Job advert in an employment agency

PLEASE DO NOT LEAN ON THE WIDOW

On a cruise ship

IN MEMORIAM

THIS TREE IS
A SYMBOL OF
OUR MUM.
PEACEFUL,
STRONG AND
SHELTERING
FROM HER
CHILDREN.

Plaque in a Midlands arboretum

WANTED

UNMARRIED

GIRLS

TO PICK FRESH

FRUIT

AND PRODUCE

AT NIGHT

On a farm

In an American maternity ward

FOR
INDOOR
OR
OUTDOOR
USE
ONLY

On a string of Chinese-made
Christmas lights

SLICED HAM WITH VEGETARIAN CHEDDAR

Pre-packed croissant label

Outside a disco

MIXING BOWL
SET DESIGNED
TO PLEASE A
COOK
WITH ROUND
BOTTOM
FOR EFFICIENT
BEATING

Sign in kitchen shop

QUICKSAND

ANY PERSON PASSING
THIS POINT WILL BE
DROWNED
BY ORDER OF THE
DISTRICT COUNCIL

Sign warning of quicksand

A BEAN SUPPER WILL BE HELD ON TUESDAY EVENING IN THE CHURCH HALL. MUSIC WILL FOLLOW.

Sign in a church

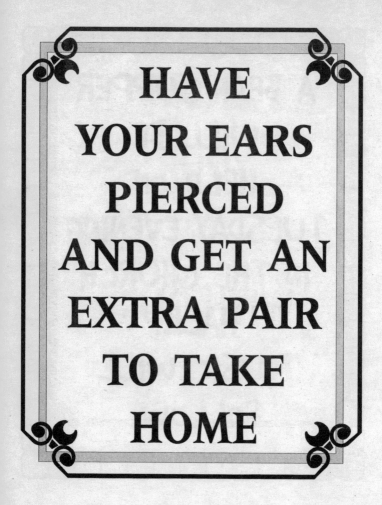

HAVE YOUR EARS PIERCED AND GET AN EXTRA PAIR TO TAKE HOME

In a jewellery shop

WE UNBLOCK YOUR CONSTIPATION WITH OUR FINGERS

Ad for an American reflexology centre

DUE TO
INCREASING
PROBLEMS
WITH LITTER LOUTS
AND VANDALS
WE MUST ASK
ANYONE WITH
RELATIVES
BURIED IN THE
GRAVEYARD
TO DO THEIR BEST
TO KEEP THEM IN
ORDER

**Notice sent to residents of a
Wiltshire parish**

ELEPHANTS PLEASE STAY IN YOUR CAR

In a safari park

WARNING: CONTAINS NUTS

On a packet of supermarket own brand peanuts

On an airline packet of peanuts

On a fast food outlet handy wipe

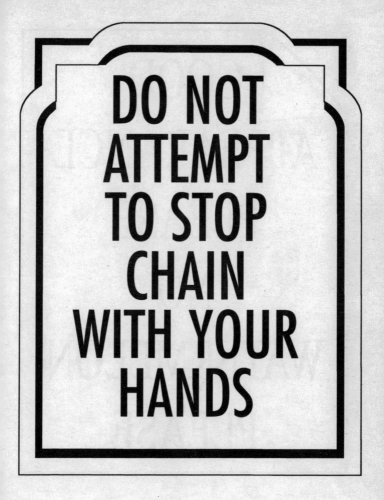

DO NOT
ATTEMPT
TO STOP
CHAIN
WITH YOUR
HANDS

On a Swedish chainsaw

GOOD APPEARANCE PLEASE NO WATERMELON PLEASE

Sign in a Beijing hotel lobby

BARGAIN
BASEMENT
UPSTAIRS

Sign in a London department store

SALE OF LOST AND UNCLAIMED PROPERTY

UMBRELLAS BY THE THOUSAND, HANDBAGS, BRIEFCASES, OVERCOATS, ABANDONED CHILDREN

Advert from lost property auction guide

DO NOT

DRIVE CAR
OR
OPERATE
MACHINERY

On a bottle of children's cough medicine

PLEASE
KEEP OUT
OF
CHILDREN

On a Korean kitchen knife

WE EXCHANGE ANYTHING

BICYCLES, WASHING MACHINES ETC WHY NOT BRING YOUR WIFE ALONG AND GET A WONDERFUL BARGAIN?

Outside a second-hand shop

NOT TO BE USED FOR THE OTHER USE

On a Japanese food processor

HORSE MANURE

50p PER PRE-PACKED BAG

20p DO-IT-YOURSELF

Outside a farm

WARNING:
MAY CAUSE
DROWSINESS

On a packet of sleeping tablets

Advert for a Jakarta shoe company

PRODUCE OF MORE THAN ONE COUNTRY

On a SINGLE pre-packaged vanilla pod in most supermarkets!

DANGER!
PUBLIC MUST NOTE, TO KILL BABIES, INSERT THEM HEAD INTO BAG. CAREFULLY! THANK YOU

From the plastic cover of a child's surfboard

AUTOMATIC WASHING MACHINES

PLEASE REMOVE ALL YOUR CLOTHES WHEN THE LIGHT GOES OUT

Sign in a launderette

```
SUITABLE
FOR
VEGETARIANS
```

**On a bottle of supermarket
mineral water**

THIS DOOR IS NOT TO BE USED AS AN EXIT OR AN ENTRANCE

Sign on door at a New York post office

NO
TRESPASSING
WITHOUT
PERMISSION

Sign on church property

PRODUCT WILL BE HOT AFTER HEATING

On pre-packaged bread pudding

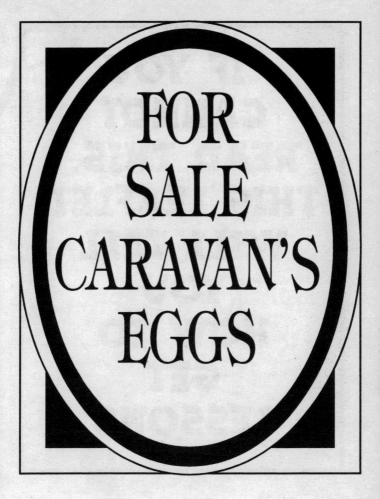

FOR SALE CARAVAN'S EGGS

By a Derbyshire roadside

IF YOU CANNOT READ THIS, THIS LEAFLET WILL TELL YOU HOW TO GET LESSONS

On a leaflet

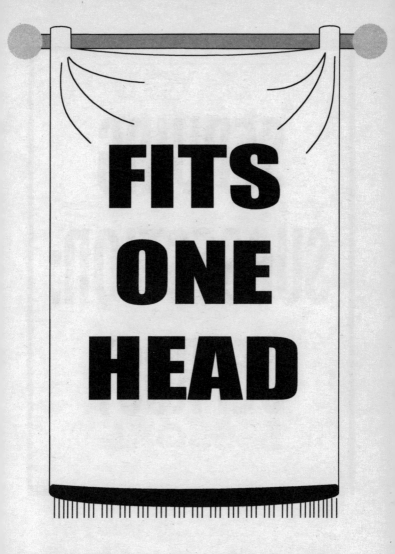

FITS ONE HEAD

On a shower cap provided by a hotel

SERVING SUGGESTION: DEFROST

On a range of frozen dinners

OUT TO
LUNCH
IF NOT
BACK BY FIVE,
OUT FOR
DINNER ALSO

Outside a photographer's studio

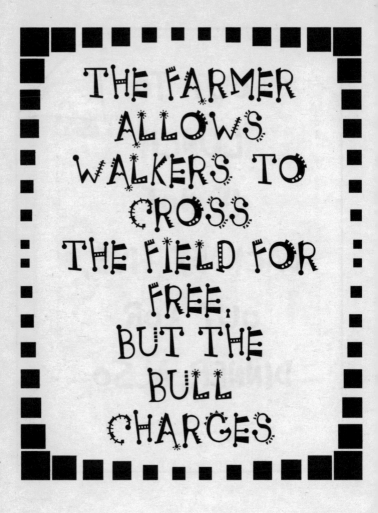

THE FARMER
ALLOWS
WALKERS TO
CROSS
THE FIELD FOR
FREE,
BUT THE
BULL
CHARGES

Notice in a field

CLOSED DUE TO ILLNESS

Notice in health food shop window

DO NOT IRON CLOTHES ON BODY

On packaging for a steam iron

FOR ANYONE
WHO HAS
CHILDREN
AND DOESN'T
KNOW IT,
THERE IS A
CRECHE
ON THE
FIRST FLOOR

Sign at a conference

DIRECTIONS: USE LIKE REGULAR SOAP

On a bar of soap

SAME DAY
DRY CLEANING
ALL
GARMENTS
READY IN
48 HOURS

In the window of a dry cleaner's

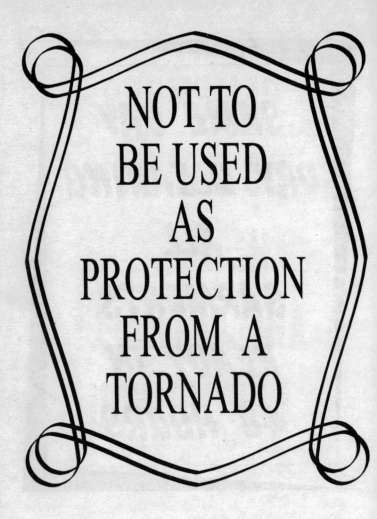

NOT TO BE USED AS PROTECTION FROM A TORNADO

On a blanket from Taiwan

REMEMBER, OBJECTS IN THE MIRROR ARE ACTUALLY BEHIND YOU

On a helmet mounted mirror used by US cyclists

DOGS FOUND WORRYING WILL BE SHOT

Sign on a farm gate

USE REPEATEDLY FOR SEVERE DAMAGE

On a Taiwanese shampoo

AFTER OPENING KEEP UPRIGHT

On the bottle-top of a flavoured milk drink

Low
SELF ESTEEM
SUPPORT GROUP
MEETS THURSDAY
AT 7PM

PLEASE USE
THE BACK DOOR

Sign in church hall

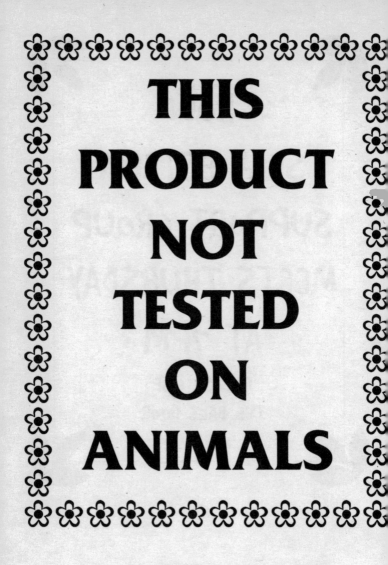

THIS PRODUCT NOT TESTED ON ANIMALS

On a New Zealand insect spray

PLEASE DO NOT FEED THE ELEPHANTS

**IF YOU HAVE
ANY PEANUTS
OR BUNS
GIVE THEM TO
THE KEEPER
ON DUTY**

At the zoo

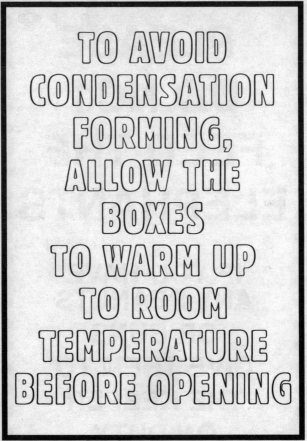

TO AVOID CONDENSATION FORMING, ALLOW THE BOXES TO WARM UP TO ROOM TEMPERATURE BEFORE OPENING

In a US guide to setting up a new computer found INSIDE the box

NO WALKING, SITTING OR PLAYING ON THE GRASS IN THIS PLEASURE PARK

Notice in a London park

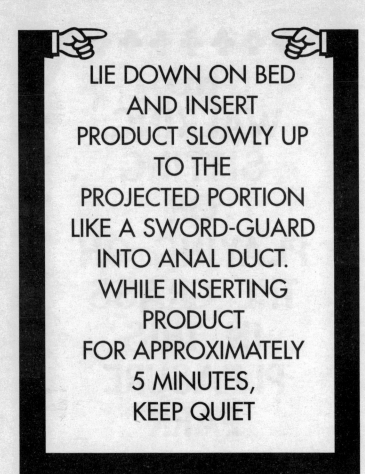

LIE DOWN ON BED
AND INSERT
PRODUCT SLOWLY UP
TO THE
PROJECTED PORTION
LIKE A SWORD-GUARD
INTO ANAL DUCT.
WHILE INSERTING
PRODUCT
FOR APPROXIMATELY
5 MINUTES,
KEEP QUIET

On a Japanese product used to relieve painful haemorrhoids

WE REPAIR
WHAT
YOUR
HUSBAND
FIXED

Sign on a repair shop door

OPEN OTHER END

**In some countries,
on the BOTTOM of cola bottles**

WHY NOT TRY TOSSING OVER YOUR FAVOURITE BREAKFAST CEREAL?

On a packet of raisins

FOR
SALE
BUY
OWNER

Private sale board outside a house

In a Mexico City hotel

EAT HERE GET GAS FREE

Outside an American service station

WARNING

REMOVE CHILD BEFORE FOLDING

On a pushchair

YOU HAVE NO REASON TO TRY OUR BEST RESTAURANT

**Sign in an Indonesian
hotel restaurant**

Sign in Japanese beauty parlour

VOLUME ON. SQUELCH. PLEASE DIAL TO SHUT WHENEVER YOU WANT TO

Sign in a Tokyo hotel bathroom

DO NOT ENTER.

PLEASE COME IN.

Signs on a door at a motel in America

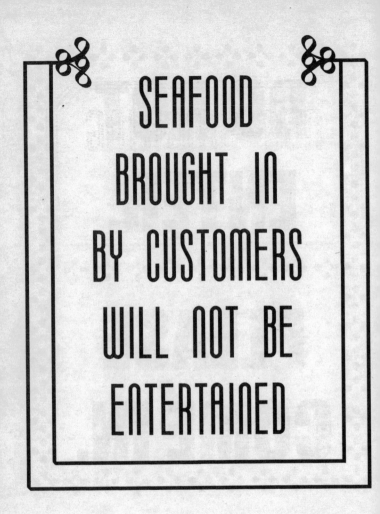

SEAFOOD
BROUGHT IN
BY CUSTOMERS
WILL NOT BE
ENTERTAINED

Sign at a restaurant in Malaysia

Sign in hotel lobby, Jordan

IT IS ADVISORY TO BE TWO PEOPLE DURING ASSEMBLY

Instructions included with a Swedish flat-packed cabinet

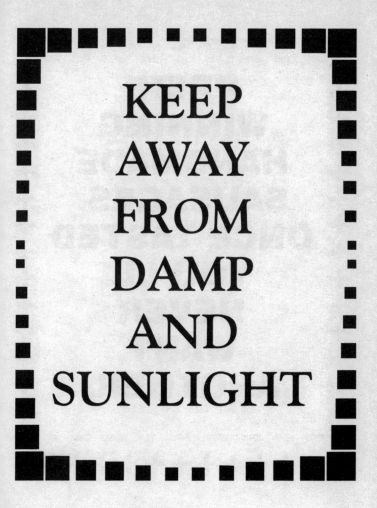

KEEP AWAY FROM DAMP AND SUNLIGHT

On a set of garden furniture

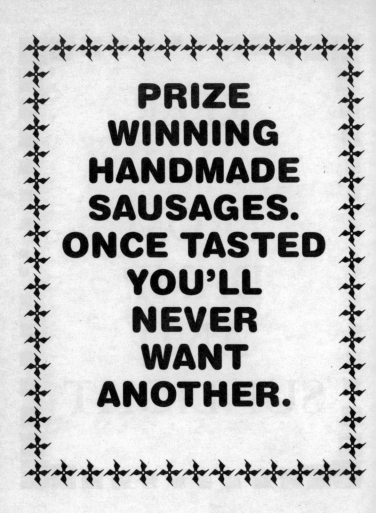

PRIZE WINNING HANDMADE SAUSAGES. ONCE TASTED YOU'LL NEVER WANT ANOTHER.

Sign at a farm shop

MINOR
SIDE-EFFECTS
INCLUDE
SNEEZING

**Safety warning on
hay fever nasal-spray remedy**

ANTIQUE TABLES MADE DAILY

Sign by a roadside in America

WARNING:

DO NOT DRIVE WHILST USING THIS PRODUCT

On a packet of condoms

JESUS IS COMING!

NO BINGO ON SUNDAY

Notice outside a US church

CAUTION:
WATER ON
ROAD
DURING RAIN

American road sign

FOR BEST RESULTS, START WITH CLEAN BATHTUB BEFORE USE

On a bottle of bathtub cleaner

DIETING GROUP WILL MEET AT 7PM AT THE FIRST PRESBYTERIAN CHURCH.

PLEASE USE LARGE DOUBLE DOOR AT THE SIDE ENTRANCE.

Notice on a church bulletin board

IF YOU GET THIS LIQUID IN YOUR EYE RINSE CAREFULLY WITH WATER

**Instructions on a bottle of
distilled water in a research laboratory**

ANY MEMBER OF STAFF WHO NEEDS TO TAKE THE DAY OFF TO GO TO A FUNERAL MUST WARN THE FOREMAN ON THE MORNING OF THE MATCH

Seen in a factory

**Advertising and instructions
on an American cereal packet**

HALF-DAY CLOSING

CLOSING

ALL DAY

WEDNESDAY

Notice on Norfolk village shop door

PLEASE MIND THE STEPS

Outside a dancing academy

TODAY'S SPECIAL POT OF TEA WITH STONES AND JAM

Sign in a tea shop

STYLIST WANTED.

GOOD PAY AND FRINGE BENEFITS. EXCELLENT GROWTH POTENTIAL.

Notice in hairdresser's window

OPEN
24 HOURS
EXCEPT
2AM-8AM

Sign in London pizza parlour

BABY SHOW

ALL ENTRIES TO BE HANDED IN AT THE GATE

Sign at a garden fête

In a café window

NO CHILDREN ALOUD

Outside a very exclusive boutique

CUSTOMERS WHO FIND OUR WAITING STAFF RUDE SHOULD SEE THE MANAGER

In a restaurant

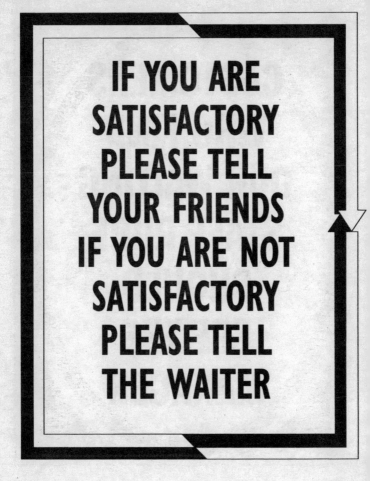

In a Chinese restaurant

TRY OUR
LOCAL BUTTER
NOBODY CAN
TOUCH IT

In a grocery shop

OUR MOTTO:
WE PROMISE
YOU THE
LOWEST
PRICES
AND
WORKMANSHIP

Outside a furniture shop

AUTO
REPAIR
SERVICE.
FREE PICK-UP
AND DELIVERY.
TRY US ONCE,
YOU'LL NEVER
GO ANYWHERE
AGAIN.

Outside a garage

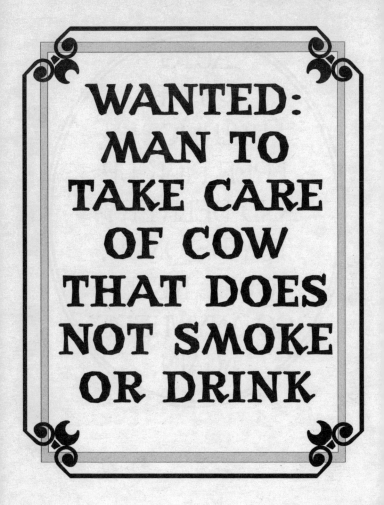

WANTED:
MAN TO
TAKE CARE
OF COW
THAT DOES
NOT SMOKE
OR DRINK

Sign on a farm

OUR BIKINIS ARE EXCITING. THEY ARE SIMPLY THE TOPS.

Advert in a dress shop window

Sign in a dry cleaner's

FOR RENT

SIX ROOM
HATED
APARTMENT

Michael O'Mara Humour

All Michael O'Mara titles are available by post from:
Bookpost, PO Box 29, Douglas, Isle of Man, IM99 1BQ

Credit cards accepted. Telephone: 01624 677237 Fax: 01624 670923
Email: bookshop@enterprise.net Internet: www.bookpost.co.uk

Free postage and packing in the UK.

Other Michael O'Mara Humour titles include:

The Book of Urban Legends	ISBN 1-85479-932-0 pb £3.99
Born for the Job	ISBN 1-84317-099-X pb £5.99
The Complete Book of Farting	ISBN 1-85479-440-X pb £4.99
The Ultimate Insult	ISBN 1-85479-288-1 pb £5.99
Wicked Cockney Rhyming Slang	ISBN 1-85479-386-1 pb £3.99
The Wicked Wit of Jane Austen	ISBN 1-85479-652-6 hb £9.99
The Wicked Wit of Winston Churchill	ISBN 1-85479-529-5 hb £9.99
The Wicked Wit of Oscar Wilde	ISBN 1-85479-542-2 hb £9.99
The World's Stupidest Laws	ISBN 1-84317-172-4 pb £4.99
The World's Stupidest Signs	ISBN 1-84317-170-8 pb £4.99
More of the World's Stupidest Signs	ISBN 1-84317-032-9 pb £4.99
The World's Stupidest Last Words	ISBN 1-84317-021-3 pb £4.99
The World's Stupidest Inventions	ISBN 1-84317-036-1 pb £5.99
The World's Stupidest Criminals	ISBN 1-84317-171-6 pb £4.99
The World's Stupidest Instructions	ISBN 1-84317-078-7 pb £4.99
The World's Stupidest Sporting Screw-Ups	ISBN 1-84317-039-6 pb £4.99
The World's Stupidest Chat-Up Lines	ISBN 1-84317-019-1 pb £4.99
The World's Stupidest Husbands	ISBN 1-84317-168-6 pb £4.99
The World's Stupidest Celebrities	ISBN 1-84317-137-6 pb £4.99
The World's Stupidest Deaths	ISBN 1-84317-136-8 pb £4.99
Cricket: It's A Funny Old Game	ISBN 1-84317-090-6 pb £4.99
Football: It's A Funny Old Game	ISBN 1-84317-091-4 pb £4.99
Laughable Latin	ISBN 1-84317-097-3 pb £4.99
School Rules	ISBN 1-84317-100-7 pb £4.99
Sex Cheques (new edition)	ISBN 1-84317-121-X pb £3.50
The Timewaster Letters	ISBN 1-84317-108-2 pb £9.99
The Jordan Joke Book	ISBN 1-84317-120-1 pb £4.99
Speak Well English	ISBN 1-84317-088-4 pb £5.99
Shite's Unoriginal Miscellany	ISBN 1-84317-064-7 hb £9.99
Eats, Shites & Leaves	ISBN 1-84317-098-1 hb £9.99
A Shite History of Nearly Everything	ISBN 1-84317-138-4 hb £9.99